LET'S FIND OUT! SPORTS

WHAT IS BASKETBALL?

SIYAVUSH SAIDIAN

Britannica
Educational Publishing
IN ASSOCIATION WITH
ROSEN
EDUCATIONAL SERVICES

Published in 2019 by Britannica Educational Publishing (a trademark of Encyclopædia Britannica, Inc.) in association with The Rosen Publishing Group, Inc.
29 East 21st Street, New York, NY 10010

Distributed exclusively by Rosen Publishing.
To see additional Britannica Educational Publishing titles, go to rosenpublishing.com.

First Edition

Britannica Educational Publishing
J.E. Luebering: Executive Director, Core Editorial
Mary Rose McCudden: Editor, Britannica Student Encyclopedia

Rosen Publishing
Brian Garvey: Series Designer/Book Layout
Cindy Reiman: Photography Manager

Library of Congress Cataloging-in-Publication Data

Names: Saidian, Siyavush, author.
Title: What is basketball? / Siyavush Saidian.
Description: First Edition. | New York : Rosen Publishing, 2019. | Series: Let's find out! Sports | "Distributed exclusively by Rosen Publishing"—T.p. verso. |
Includes webography. | Includes bibliographical references and index. | Audience: Grades 1-5 |
Identifiers: LCCN 2018026729| ISBN 9781538304747 (library bound) | ISBN 9781538304785 (paperback) | ISBN 9781538304877 (6 pack)
Subjects: LCSH: Basketball—Juvenile literature. | Basketball—United States—History—Juvenile literature.
Classification: LCC GV885.1 .S24 2019 | DDC 796.3230973—dc23
LC record available at https://lccn.loc.gov/2018026729

Manufactured in the United States of America

Photo credits: Cover, interior pages background Eugene Onischenko/Shutterstock.com; p. 4 Tim Warner/Getty Images; p. 5 MB Media/Getty Images; p. 6 © Encyclopædia Britannica, Inc.; p. 7 Brocreative/Shutterstock.com; p. 8 Dean Drobot/Shutterstock.com; p. 9 Greg Nelson/Sports Illustrated/Getty Images; p. 10 Felix Mizioznikov/Shutterstock.com; p. 11 Randy Belice/National Basketball Association/Getty Images; pp. 12, 22 Aspen Photo/Shutterstock.com; p. 13 Pavel Shchegolev/Shutterstock.com; p. 14 Anthony Au-Yeung/Getty Images; p. 15 Ezra Shaw/Getty Images; p. 16 Rawpixel.com/Shutterstock.com; p. 17 Portland Press Herald/Getty Images; p. 18 © UPI/Bettmann Archive; p. 19 J and L Photography/Getty Images; p. 20 Zhang Peng/LightRocket/Getty Images; p. 21 Focus On Sport/Getty Images; p. 23 Brett Wilhelm/NCAA Photos/Getty Images; p. 24 NCAA Photos/Getty Images; p. 25 Oleksandr Osipov/Shutterstock.com; p. 26 © Dick Raphael; p. 27 Tinseltown/Shutterstock.com; p. 28 Andy Lyons/Getty Images; p. 29 A.Ricardo/Shutterstock.com.

Contents

Shooting Hoops

Basketball is a fast-paced and exciting sport. It is very popular in the United States, where it was first played in the 1890s. It has also become popular in many other countries. In a basketball game, two teams of five players compete. The goal is to score more points than the other team. Players score by tossing—or shooting—a ball through a raised goal called a basket, or hoop.

Basketball has always enjoyed great popularity. Within a decade

There is always someone moving on the basketball court, which makes games quick and entertaining.

Many countries outside the United States have their own professional basketball leagues.

VOCABULARY

Athletic **circuits** are leagues of teams that compete against each other.

of its invention there were women's teams, professional circuits, and college leagues. The game quickly spread to Canada, Europe, and Australia. Today, young people play basketball in grade school, high school, college, and at athletic clubs. In addition to amateur teams, there are professional leagues and independent professional clubs throughout the world.

PLAYING AREA AND EQUIPMENT

The dimensions of a basketball court are 50 feet (15.2 meters) by 94 feet (28.7 m) for professional and college play. There is a line that divides the court in half, and in the middle is the center circle. Another court marking is the three-point line. It is 20 feet, 9 inches (6.3 m) from the basket for college players. In the US men's professional league, it is 23 feet, 9 inches (7.2 m).

Every basketball court used for professional games in the United States has the same dimensions.

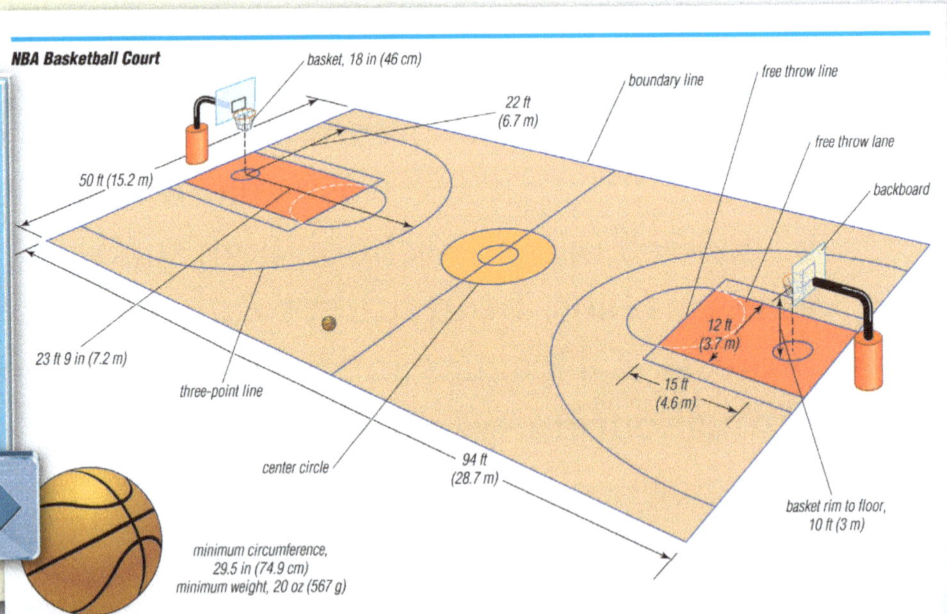

The orange metal hoop and white net are among the most well-known parts of a basketball court.

At each end of the court is a basket 10 feet (3 m) above the floor. The basket is an orange metal ring with an open net hanging from the rim.

Players wear sleeveless jerseys and athletic shorts. This loose clothing helps players run, jump, and shoot. Basketball shoes are thicker and heavier than running shoes. They help players jump and change directions.

A basketball team has five players: two forwards, two guards, and a center. The players at each position have special skills and tasks. For example, guards are good at moving the ball down the court and passing it to teammates.

THINK ABOUT IT

Why do you think basketball players do not wear padded uniforms?

Playing the Game

Basketball players play both offense and defense. When a team has the ball, it is on offense and tries to score points. The other team plays defense. It tries to keep the opposing team from scoring. It also tries to gain control of the ball.

The only way to score points in a basketball game is to throw, or shoot, the ball through the hoop.

Play begins with a jump ball. A referee tosses up the ball between two opposing players in the middle of the court. The two players jump for the ball and try to tap it to a teammate. The other players stand outside the center circle. The team that gets control of the ball plays offense first.

Compare and Contrast

What makes offense and defense alike in basketball? What makes them different?

The tip-off, or jump ball, is used to determine who begins play on offense.

Being able to dribble the ball is one of a player's most important skills.

The offensive team tries to advance the ball toward the defensive team's basket. Offensive players can pass the ball to teammates. They can also move the ball down the court by themselves. To move the ball, players must dribble, or bounce, the ball on the court as they run with it.

Any player with the ball may take a shot at the basket. Most successful shots score two points. Shots from behind the three-point line score three points.

Think About It

Basketball players must dribble if they want to advance the ball. How does that make the game different from other sports?

The team on defense tries to stop the offense's shots. When a shot is missed, both teams try to recover—or rebound—the ball. If the offense rebounds the ball, it can try to take another shot. If the defense gets the rebound, it becomes the offense. The defense can also take away—or steal—the ball from the offense during a pass or a dribble.

Defensive players are always trying to make a play on the ball, such as the one shown here.

FOULS

A group of officials makes sure that the players follow the rules of the game. The officials penalize a team when one of its players breaks a rule. For example, if an offensive player runs without dribbling the ball, the officials give the ball to the defense.

Some penalties are called personal fouls. Most fouls happen when one player

Players are not allowed to stop a ball from going in the basket, but they can try to block an opponent from shooting the ball.

Think About It

Why are there different kinds of penalties in basketball?

A player who is awarded a free throw is allowed to shoot the ball without any interference from the opposing players.

makes physical contact with another player. For example, officials call fouls for bumping, pushing, and tripping. The player who is fouled often gets to take shots without having to worry about the defense. These shots are called free throws. They score one point each. For some fouls the opposing team is given the ball and allowed to throw it in from out of bounds. If a player has too many personal fouls he or she must leave the game.

STYLES OF PLAY

Teams use different styles of play on both offense and defense. One of the best-known styles of offensive play is the motion offense. In the motion offense, players move in and out of the area in front of the basket, trying to confuse defenders. A common play within the motion offense is the pick-and-roll. In this play, an offensive

Pick-and-roll plays are among the most common strategies in basketball, from youth to professional leagues.

player sets a "pick" for a teammate with the ball by getting in the way of a defender. If the defender follows the ball handler, the other player moves, or "rolls," toward the basket and can get open for a pass and shot.

There are two main styles of defense—zone and man-to-man. In a zone defense, each defensive player guards one area on the court. In man-to-man defense, each player guards an assigned player on the opposing team.

Compare and Contrast

What makes zone and man-to-man defenses similar? What makes them different?

A man-to-man defense typically creates matchups between each team's best players.

YOUTH BASKETBALL

One reason basketball has become so popular is that people of all ages can play it. There are many youth basketball leagues, often run by schools or local organizations. Most of the rules of the game are the same, even for very young players. However, there are also some differences.

In youth basketball games, the court is typically smaller than the court that professional players use. Another difference is that

In youth basketball, the lower hoop makes it easier for players to score points and shoot comfortably.

Think About It

Why do you think youth basketball leagues have different rules?

Press defense is good for taking the ball away from an offense, but it is usually not allowed in youth leagues.

the hoop is lower to the ground. The three-point and free-throw lines are also closer to the hoop. There are often special rules in place to prevent player injuries. Some leagues do not allow zone defense because players can bump into each other more easily. Press defense is also not allowed. In this type of defense, defenders play very close to offensive players, which can lead to injury.

History

James Naismith invented basketball in 1891. Naismith was a physical education teacher in Springfield, Massachusetts. His school asked him to create a sport that students could play indoors during the winter. The first basketball game used peach baskets as the goals. That is why the sport was named basketball. In early games of basketball, officials had to climb ladders to remove

James Naismith, shown here, named his new sport after the fact that it originally used real baskets as the goals.

Think About It

How do you think removing baskets and adding hoops has improved basketball?

Since the mid-1900s, basketball has been selling out arenas all across the United States.

the ball each time a team had a successful shot. The metal hoop was not invented until 1906.

Basketball quickly became popular throughout the United States. Both men and women started playing basketball at the college level in the early 1890s. The first professional basketball league in the United States was formed in 1898. The National Basketball Association (NBA) started in 1949. The Women's National Basketball Association (WNBA) began in 1997.

The NBA

The NBA was formed in the United States in 1949 by the merger of two rival organizations: the National Basketball League and the Basketball Association of America.

By the early 1980s, the NBA had low attendance, bad television ratings, and teams that were losing money. The league improved when David Stern became the NBA

Vocabulary

Television ratings measure how successful a television program is.

The NBA has overcome many challenges to become one of the most popular professional sports leagues in the United States.

commissioner in 1984. Stern helped make basketball more popular. The amazing talents of several players at the time also helped make the game more entertaining. Those superstars included Magic Johnson, Larry Bird, and Michael Jordan.

Today the NBA is made up of thirty teams, split into two conferences. The Eastern Conference and the Western Conference each has three divisions. The best teams at the end of each season participate in a championship tournament. The NBA Finals are played between the best teams from the Eastern and Western Conferences.

Magic Johnson was one of the best players in the 1980s.

March Madness

In addition to the NBA, college basketball is a very popular sport in the United States. The National Collegiate Athletic Association (NCAA) holds a men's and a women's tournament each year in March for the best teams in the country. The tournament is often called March Madness.

March Madness features the best college basketball teams from all over the country.

The first NCAA men's basketball tournament was held

in 1939, but the tournament did not become popular until the 1960s. At first, only eight teams were allowed to participate. Now, each year there are sixty-eight teams that play for the men's championship. The teams are split into four divisions. Within each division the teams are paired up to form the tournament **bracket**.

Becoming the national champion team is the goal of all sixty-eight participants in March Madness.

Many fans like to fill out the bracket before the tournament starts by guessing who will win each game.

VOCABULARY

A **bracket** is the list of match-ups in a tournament.

Basketball Around the World

Outside the United States, basketball developed more slowly. Men's basketball became an Olympic event in 1936. A friend of James Naismith named Forrest C. Allen helped convince the Olympics to include basketball. He wanted to increase its global popularity. International world championships began in 1950 for men and in 1953 for women. Women's basketball was added to the Olympics in 1976.

Forrest C. Allen, shown here, was a big part of bringing basketball to an international audience.

The International Basketball Federation (FIBA) is in charge of making rules for international games. The NBA and FIBA rules are similar, but there are some important differences. For example, FIBA games are eight minutes shorter. Each quarter is two minutes shorter than in NBA games. In addition, the three-point line in the NBA is farther back, which makes it harder to score three points.

Think About It

Why are there different rules for different people if they are playing the same game?

FIBA is the organization in charge of making rules and supervising most international leagues and games.

Famous Players

New basketball fans may believe that current players are the greatest, but many older players are among the best of all time. One of the best players from earlier days is Bill Russell. He played for the Boston Celtics from 1956 to 1969, winning eleven championships during that time. No other player has won as many championships as Russell. He was named the NBA's most valuable player (MVP) five times. Russell was elected

Many experts believe no one will ever win more championships than Bill Russell.

Think About It

Why do you think early NBA players had so much success?

to the Naismith Memorial Basketball Hall of Fame in 1975.

When he retired in 1989, Kareem Abdul-Jabbar held several records, including the record for the most points scored. It is a record he still holds. He led the Los Angeles Lakers to five championship victories between 1980 and 1988. Abdul-Jabbar also earned the NBA MVP award six times. In 1995, he was elected to the Hall of Fame.

Kareem Abdul-Jabbar was awarded the Presidential Medal of Freedom in 2016 for his work on and off the basketball court.

One of the best and most famous players of all time is Michael Jordan. He played for the Chicago Bulls for many years, breaking nearly every NBA record during his career. The Bulls won the NBA championship six times during his career. Jordan won five MVP awards. He was elected to the Hall of Fame in 2009.

Jordan earned the nickname "Air Jordan" because of his leaping ability. After he retired he lent his name to several very succesful products, including Air Jordan basketball shoes.

Outside of basketball, Michael Jordan is known for his partnership with Nike and the "Jumpman" logo.

LeBron James entered the NBA in 2003 and quickly became one of the league's superstars. An extremely talented forward, James was selected as the NBA's MVP in 2009, 2010, 2012, and 2013. James was only the tenth player in NBA history to have earned that honor in back-to-back seasons. In 2017 he set a record for postseason points, passing Michael Jordan.

LeBron James is among the greats because he is good at both offense and defense.

Vocabulary

The **postseason** is when the NBA's top teams play each other to reach the championship.

GLOSSARY

advance To move forward.

amateur A person who takes part in an activity for pleasure and not for pay.

championship A contest held to find a champion.

collegiate Of or relating to a college.

commissioner An official in charge of a sports league.

conference An association of athletic teams.

confuse To trick or mix up.

dimensions The range over which something extends.

divide To separate into two or more parts or pieces.

elect To select by vote for an office, position, or membership.

fast-paced Describing a high speed of play with a lot of movement.

inflated Filled with air or gas.

injury Hurt, damage, or loss received.

merger The combination of two or more companies into one.

Olympics A series of international athletic contests held in a different country during the summer and the winter once every four years.

penalize To give a penalty to.

pick When an offensive player prevents a defensive player from guarding.

rebound To gain possession of a basketball after a missed shot.

referee A sports official usually having final authority in conducting a game.

retire To give up one's job.

zone An area on a playing field.

For More Information

Books

Bodden, Valerie. *LeBron James: Champion Basketball Star*. Minneapolis, MN: ABDO Publishing, 2014.

Clausen-Grace, Nicki, and Jeff Grace. *Basketball Science*. Mankato, MN: Black Rabbit Books, 2018.

Ervin, Phil. *Basketball Trivia*. Minneapolis, MN: SportsZone, 2016.

Lindeen, Mary. *Let's Play Basketball*. Chicago, IL: Norwood House, 2016.

Nagelhout, Ryan. *Basketball: Who Does What?* New York, NY: Gareth Stevens, 2018.

Websites

Basketball Reference
www.basketball-reference.com
Twitter: @bball_ref;
Facebook, Instagram:
@Basketball.Reference

HoopsHype
www.hoopshype.com
Twitter, Facebook: @HoopsHype

Naismith Memorial Basketball Hall of Fame
www.hoophall.com
Twitter, Instagram: @Hoophall;
Facebook: @BBHOF

National Basketball Association
www.nba.com
Twitter, Facebook, Instagram: @NBA

Index